Boscobel House

Nicola Stacey

Introduction

Boscobel House, a handsome 17th-century timber-framed lodge, was built by John Giffard, a local landowner from Chillington in Staffordshire. Hidden in deep woodland, the house was given a consciously romantic name: Boscobel, from 'bosco bello', or 'beautiful wood'. Giffard was a Catholic, and his new house was well suited to hiding Catholics, who needed refuge from religious persecution. For a few days in 1651, the house played a pivotal role in English history, as the hiding place of the future King Charles II (r.1660–85). Fleeing after the battle of Worcester, Charles was brought in secret first to White Ladies, a former priory nearby, and then to Boscobel. Here he was cared for by the five Penderel brothers, loyal servants of the Giffards, who risked their lives to protect him. Charles hid in an oak tree at Boscobel with his officer, William Careless, and a descendant of the Royal Oak still stands near the house today.

The story of Boscobel and the Royal Oak became famous immediately after the Restoration in 1660, and it has brought visitors to the house ever since. In the 19th century, the house was bought by a Derbyshire industrialist, Walter Evans, and the farmyard was rebuilt in line with new ideas of agricultural efficiency. Evans and his family also refurbished the house's interior in an 'antiquarian' style, inspired by the story of Charles's visit. The house today reflects all these many layers. It is a unique and charming place, which has captured the public imagination for almost 400 years.

Above: Portrait of Charles II after the Restoration in 1660, painted by Sir Peter Lely

Facing page: Aerial view of Boscobel with the Royal Oak in the foreground

Tour

Hidden within Boscobel's dramatic black and white exterior is a modest, late 16th-century house. Visitors enter first through a 19th-century wing, then pass through the early house to reach the later 17th-century lodge, now refurnished as it was around 1900. Leaving the lodge and entering the garden, visitors can reach the Royal Oak, at the end of a short trail beyond the garden gate. The farm buildings, furnished as they were in the 19th century, can be seen at the end of the tour. The former priory of White Ladies is a pleasant walk along a path from the Royal Oak, or one mile down the public road.

FOLLOWING THE TOUR

The tour starts in the house. The numbers beside the headings highlight the key points on the tour and correspond with the small numbered plans in the margins.

OVERVIEW OF BOSCOBEL

Despite looking architecturally coherent, Boscobel is not all it seems to be. A closer inspection of the building reveals that some of the 'timbers' are in fact painted brick – a 19th-century attempt to disguise a later extension. The oldest part of the house, now called the north range, consists of the inner two bays of the long low wing. Dating from the 16th century, this early building was later extended and its ground floor now houses the 19th-century dairy. Behind the north range is the most impressive part of the house: the tall, timber-framed lodge built some time before 1624. There is an introductory display on the history of Boscobel in the 19th-century farmhouse wing. The original entrance to the lodge, still accessible today, is via the garden.

The farm buildings all date from the 19th century, except for the long timber-framed barn, which survives from the 17th-century farmyard. The farmhouse, painted to appear timber-framed, dates from the late 18th century. It is now private accommodation. The cowhouse, underneath the granary, houses the estate office.

■ ENTRANCE HALL

The entrance hall at Boscobel (beyond the introductory display) is one of the oldest parts of the house. This room formed the western bay of a two-bayed late 16th-century house (see drawing **A** on page 6). Study of its timber-framing suggests that this bay may originally have been open to the roof, while the eastern bay next door was floored. The two bays were divided by a large smoke-hood, a primitive kind of

Above: Boscobel House seen from the farmyard. The 18th-century farmhouse is on the right and the 17th-century lodge at the back
Below: The entrance hall looking north-east, showing the late 16th-century timber framing

Facing page: Boscobel's striking chimney stack. The decorative painted windows appear to be an original feature and occur in 17th-century illustrations, although this exact design dates from the 19th century

The Development of Boscobel House

A *The earliest building at Boscobel in about 1595*

B *Boscobel after 1624*

C *Boscobel in about 1796, with an extended north range*

D *Boscobel in about 1820*

chimney, which was set on the other side of the facing wall. It was a modest building and its knotted and gnarled timbers and rough wattle and daub are visible in the exposed panel.

Some time before 1624 the new lodge was built up against this earlier building, and the rooms and spaces were reconfigured (see drawing **B**, left). What is now the entrance hall would have allowed access to the lodge. The bay appears to have been floored over around this time, possibly with timbers from a dismantled part of the building. A new chamber, lit by a window at upper level, was created above.

By the 19th century, the ground-floor room had been subdivided to create a small entrance hall for the lodge, in front of the door, and a back parlour for the farmhouse. An inventory notes that a map of Shropshire hung on the wall on rollers, alongside other practical items such as a pedestal barometer and a fire pump. The internal walls, as well as the first floor itself, were stripped back in the late 20th century to reveal the structure of the building. The door under the gallery rail leads to the lodge cellar, where the original kitchens were sited.

THE 17TH-CENTURY LODGE

Some time before 1624, John Giffard built his new lodge. Although he became known as 'John Giffard of Boscobel', Giffard may have intended to use his new house as a country retreat rather than his main family residence. By 1626, he had inherited from his mother a larger house nearby at White Ladies, as well as other properties in the area. His new lodge was built of higher quality materials than the earlier 16th-century farmhouse. Its timbers were from top quality oak, well formed and finished; it had oak panelling and comfortable interiors. It also had some striking and unusual features, such as an imposing chimney-stack and a projecting turret. Set deep in woodland, it would have been something of a hidden curiosity.

In the 18th century Boscobel was owned by the Fitzherbert family, descendants of the Giffards. During this period it was tenanted out. There were some alterations around this time: the room upstairs was divided in two, the gabled dormers were removed from attic level, and two extensions were built to the north and the east (see drawing **C**), but the main lodge retained the same footprint.

When Boscobel was bought by Walter Evans in 1812, the family decided to return the house to its 17th-century appearance. They redecorated the rooms and acquired period furnishings and some commemorative pieces. Most of these were subsequently lost from the house, but using an inventory and photographs from about 1900, the rooms have been returned to their appearance at this date, just before its final sale (see drawing **D**).

2 PARLOUR

The parlour was the main room of the house. Its size and layout have remained unchanged since the 17th century, although the furnishings are largely Victorian. It was into this room that Charles was brought on a damp September evening in 1651, tired and in low spirits. He dined, warmed his feet and had his shoes dried before the fire. In the 17th century, the table would have been set down the middle of the room, but during the 19th century the occupants gathered chairs around the fire, as today, for warmth and conviviality.

The oak panelling is original to the house, although it has been altered to fit around the later fire surround and the bookcase on the east wall. The plaster frieze around the top covers an earlier 17th-century frieze, which was discovered during restoration work in the 1970s. The fireplace was

Below: The parlour at Boscobel. The 'Gothick' sash windows are a 19th-century replacement of the original casements

rebuilt in the early 19th century by the Evans family to commemorate Charles's visit in 1651. The three scenes engraved into the black marble tell the story of Charles's escape. The original 17th-century fireplace was of red herringbone brick, with a larger opening. It appears to have been decorated with heraldic emblems. The windows, both here and upstairs, are 19th-century 'Gothick' replacements of the original 17th-century casements. The long dining table is early 18th-century, but very similar to the original table, which remained in the house until its sale at auction in 1913. On the table is a copy of Thomas Blount's account of Charles's escape, published in 1660.

The late 17th-century painting of Charles II and early 18th-century painting of Oliver Cromwell are similar to those displayed in the parlour by the Evans family. The Evans's painting of Charles originally hung over the fireplace.

Most other furnishings in the parlour are from the 19th century: the chaise longue, chintz-covered armchair, green glass oil lamp and German oak display cabinet. The Turkey carpet and hearthrug date from the early 20th century.

Above: 17th-century Dutch portrait of a lady, on display in the parlour
Below: The parlour fireplace, rebuilt in the 19th century with three black marble engraved panels, depicting Charles's visit to Boscobel

19th-century Romanticism

Walter Evans's purchase of the Boscobel and White Ladies estate in 1812 was inspired not only by its fertile land, but by its unique and fascinating link with English history. The Evans family immediately embarked on a project to restore the house to 'as it was when Charles was there'. Their enthusiasm was encouraged by early 19th-century 'Romantic' ideals.

Beginning in the late 18th and early 19th centuries, Romanticism was an intellectual and philosophical movement that influenced literature, art and, later, architecture. In many respects the story of Boscobel epitomized many of the Romantic ideals. The Penderel brothers risking their lives for the king evoked the nobility and courage that were idealized in the Romantics' notion of the lower classes. The story of the king's escape illustrated his daring and strength of mind – heroic ideals in the early 19th century. The curiosities of Boscobel House itself – timber-framed in the old-fashioned style – would have appealed to the Romantics' interest in authentic medieval art. To a large degree, Romanticism was a nationalistic movement, looking to the glories of a nation's past. Boscobel and its preservation of the English royal line symbolized all that this entailed.

As the 19th century progressed, several novelists elaborated on the story of the fleeing king, with the appearance in 1872 of William Harrison Ainsworth's story *Boscobel, or the Royal Oak*, following the more loosely based novels *Brambletye House*, by Horatio Smith, and *Woodstock*, by Sir Walter Scott, written in 1826.

> The story of Boscobel epitomized many of the Romantic ideals

Above: A letter sent from Boscobel by J W Evans in 1891, using Gothic-style notepaper with a Royal Oak motif
Below: The Return of Charles II, by Alfred Barron Clay, painted in 1867. The subject of the Restoration was popular in Victorian times

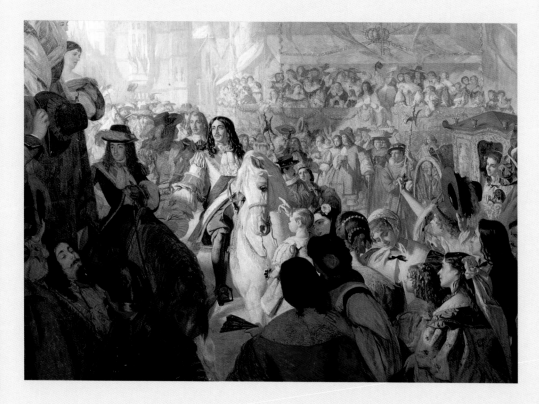

Above: The Oratory. The tapestries date from the 16th century (on the left) and the late 17th century (on the right) and are very similar to the ones here in the 19th century

Below: A detail of the carved oak chest, once belonging to the Evans family. The carcass of the chest dates from the late 17th century, while the panelling is 19th-century

3 ORATORY

This is perhaps the most puzzling room in the house. Part of the original structure of the building, it forms the ground floor of a timber-framed multangular projection. The opening onto the garden is original, but as a window only, not a door. The fireplace was inserted most probably in the 18th century, when a new kitchen was built outside with its own large chimney-stack. The door from the parlour is original, but the alcove to the left has been much altered and may hide an older entrance. The walls have been carefully painted – most likely first in the 19th century – to simulate oak panelling, and the room shows no sign of any original panelling.

At the end of the 19th century this room was called 'the oratory', perhaps after a fanciful story of Charles's visit, published in 1872, which told of William Penderel opening up a secret recess to show Charles a small altar. It is possible, however, that this room was originally the ground floor of a stair turret, with a circular stair which wound up from the ground to the first floor. If it existed, it had been removed by the late 18th century.

The commemorative carved oak chest, which has been in this room from the early 19th century, is made partly of 17th-century wood, reputedly from the original Royal Oak. The verdure tapestries are Flemish – the larger one dates from the 16th century and the smaller one from the late 17th century; they are similar to those displayed here by the Evans family. Their verdant wooded scenes are especially appropriate for Boscobel, which once lay in deep woodland.

The painting of Dame Joan Penderel above the fireplace is a 20th-century copy of a 17th-century original.

4 STAIRCASE

The staircase to the first floor is late 18th-century, although a simple stair may have been sited here from the 17th century onwards. The first landing leads to the upper floor of the north range. The window on the second landing offers the best view of the commemorative inscription laid in white cobbles by the youngest Evans daughter, Ellen, soon after the family bought the house. Written in Latin, it translates as: 'On 7 September 1651, in this house Charles II obtained the protection of five brothers of the Penderel family, and by means of their help safely escaped' (see page 15).

5 SQUIRE'S ROOM

The Squire's Room (presumably its original name) was once the main bedroom of the house. It was once larger – the same size as the parlour below. Probably during the 18th century it was divided up to create a separate bedroom next door. Well lit and heated, the Squire's Room offered views over the garden and woods beyond. It remained the main bedroom in the house, although by the late 19th century the family seldom stayed here and it was kept mostly for show. When Boscobel was sold in 1918, the room was furnished for two, with two narrow four-poster beds and a pair of washstands.

A door beside the fireplace leads into a small chamber, which is one of Boscobel's 'secret places'. In the 17th century this little room may have served as a closet for a close-stool. Below was a trapdoor, from which stairs are recorded as leading down to a small door at the bottom of the chimney-stack. This unusual feature may have been designed to allow a

First floor

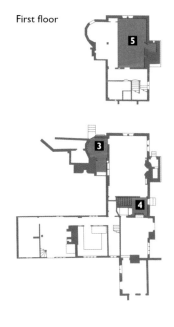

Below: The Squire's Room, showing the open closet door beside the bed, leading into one of Boscobel's 'secret places'

Above: Two plaster heads set into the frieze in the White Room. The figures wear styles fashionable in the 17th century, and may originally have been located above the fireplace in the parlour

Below: The White Room, showing the timber post which marks the original edge of the Squire's Room. The plaster heads are just visible above the panelling

fugitive to escape directly into the garden. It is likely that during the 19th century the present and more obvious 'hiding hole' was created by adding an internal floor beneath the trapdoor. The panelling is a later addition to the chamber, probably also added in the 19th century.

Close inspection of the panelling in the Squire's Room reveals other later alterations. Part of the eastern panelled wall has no carved frieze, as this section of panelling has been moved from the room next door. The window behind the bed was blocked in the late 18th century. The fireplace was decorated with delftware tiles during the 19th century.

⬛ WHITE ROOM

The White Room was created by dividing the Squire's Room next door. It was called the White Room because of its 19th-century white-painted furniture and bed coverings. The fixings for the old wattle-and-daub wall, removed to create a doorway, are still visible by the door frame.

The thick oak post in the centre of the room is original to the structure of the house and marks the original outer edge of the Squire's Room. The fireplace has been opened up in what was a small closet. The multangular projection on the east side of the room reflects the shape of the oratory below; the panelling here is not original to this space. This is possibly where the original stair came up from the ground floor. The window does not appear in early views of the house, and was probably inserted when the room was divided.

Most of the plaster frieze was added when the room was divided but the two plaster heads and two armorials are very likely 17th-century. The female head has bare bosoms rising above her dress in a style fashionable in the early 17th century, while the male head to her right is 'Roman' in style, which was also typical of the 17th century. It is possible that they were moved here during the alterations.

Attic

First floor

7 HOUSEMAID'S CUPBOARD

Tucked behind the door to the attic stairs is a small storeroom, now housing various Victorian household items. The 1913 house inventory lists tin baths and water cans in this room, as, without bathrooms, Boscobel's occupants would have had to bathe in their bedrooms, with hot water brought up from downstairs by the maid.

8 ATTIC

The stairs to the attic are the original, 17th-century stairs, although they once turned left rather than right at the top. Inside the stair cupboard, they can be seen twisting left and disappearing under the eaves, where there was once a gable on the west face of the house. These early gables, on either side of the long attic, had been removed by the end of the 18th century, along with a dormer window in the Bower Room at the far end.

Above: The housemaid's cupboard, furnished as it would have been in 1913

Below: A 19th-century engraving showing a Victorian visitor trying out the attic hiding place. The image is in reverse – an error in the printing process

The attic contains the second of Boscobel's 'secret places', just at the top of the stairs. This is most likely to have been Charles's hiding place, for it fits well with Thomas Blount's 1660 description: 'His majesty got up early (his dormitory being none of the best, nor his bed the easiest), and, near the secret place where he lay, had the convenience of a gallery to walk in, where he was observed to spend some time in his devotions, and where he had the advantage of a window, which surveyed the road from Tong to Brewood.'

During the 19th century the attic was converted to provide further accommodation. The old spinning wheel used by Dame Joan Penderel stood in the main room (the present one is a replacement). The Bower Room at the south end was used as a bedroom and the wall-paintings were added in the 19th century as a reflection on the Catholic associations of the house. They depict the Madonna lily (a symbol of purity), perhaps the Garden of Eden, and the Tree of Life.

Above: Two types of santolina growing in the garden at Boscobel: Santolina chamaecyparissus *(cotton lavender) and* Santolina rosmarinifolis

Right: View of Boscobel garden, with the mount and arbour, where Charles is said to have read on Sunday morning, 7 September 1651. The parterre beds in the 17th century would have been less elaborate

GARDEN AND EXTERIOR
OF BOSCOBEL HOUSE

Visitors can reach the garden from the farmyard through the red-brick garden wall. The garden was carefully illustrated in the first published engraving of Boscobel in 1660 (see page 25) and although it may have been embellished because of its dominance in the picture, it is still typical of a garden for this type of house in the 17th century. Rectangular parterre beds were laid out in front of a small prospect mound, on top of which was 'a pretty arbour'. Charles is said to have spent a few hours reading here in 1651, after his night spent in hiding, and 'commended the place for its retiredness'.

By the late 18th century, the garden had been reduced in size, as the land around the house was turned over to new crops. In 1790 it was described as 'a pretty large kitchen-garden planted with nut-hedges, currant and gooseberry bushes', and illustrations show horses grazing up to the door.

When the Evans family bought Boscobel in 1812, they set out to restore the garden, taking 'the old prints of the place for a pattern'. They planted new hedging and enclosed the garden to the east with a high brick wall. The beds were restored, the arbour was rebuilt, and Ellen Evans, Walter's youngest daughter, laid out a cobble inscription in front of the house, recording the king's sanctuary and escape. Her sister later recalled, 'she was not much above twenty and much enjoyed the work'. The family spent their summers here, and photographs show them enjoying the sunshine on the grass (see page 38).

The house itself was altered too: the timber-framed exterior was rendered over and the earlier porch removed. Curious features, such as the painted chimney windows, were repainted, reflecting earlier illustrations which show windows here. The small door in the side of the chimney-stack probably dates from the 17th century; later photographs show King George VI (r.1936–52) being shown inside the cramped little space his ancestor may once have had occasion to use.

Since the 1950s, the garden has been carefully restored. Box, santolina and old species of lavender, pears and apples have been planted, all of which were popular in the 17th century. Native honeysuckle has been planted in the nut walk.

Above: *The house seen from the garden, with delphiniums in bloom*
Below: *A crown marked out in cobbles to commemorate Charles's visit to Boscobel. The Latin inscription beside it reads: 'Sext Id Sept 1651 in hac domo Carolus Secundus tutela quinque fratrum de stirpe Penderel potitus est, eorumdemque ope incolumis evasit' (translated on page 11)*

Above: A delftware plaque, painted with a bust of Charles II in the Royal Oak, and made between about 1660 and 1670. The frame is reputedly made with wood from the oak itself. Many souvenirs, including snuff boxes and toys, were fashioned from the bark, wood and eventually even the roots of the tree

Below: The Royal Oak, with Boscobel House in the background

THE ROYAL OAK

In the 17th century Boscobel was a remote lodge in dense woodland. John Giffard named his house after this 'bosco bello' or 'beautiful wood', but it was also a managed woodland. Accounts of Charles's visit to Boscobel mention the practice of pollarding, or cutting down the crown structure of a tree so that the new branches can be harvested. When Charles got up 'into a great oak' in the woods near Boscobel, he chose one 'in a pretty plain place' – a small clearing – 'that had been lopped some three or four years before, and being grown out again, very bushy and thick, could not be seen through'.

After the Restoration in 1660, the oak attracted many visitors, both the curious and the reverent. Perhaps remembering the tradition of medieval relics, 17th-century visitors to the oak plucked off twigs and branches as souvenirs. Slowly the tree was denuded, and by 1680 its owners, Basil and Jane Fitzherbert, had built a protective brick wall around it. The tree, however, continued to decline, most likely further damaged by the wall's restriction of moisture to its roots. In 1712, the antiquarian William Stukeley reported that it had been 'almost cut away by travellers', but that growing 'close by the side was a young thriving plant from one of its acorns'. By 1791 only the younger tree was noted, and it seems that about this time the last roots of the earlier tree were grubbed up.

The Royal Oak today is the younger tree fully grown, but was itself damaged by storms in 2000. A replacement, grown from an acorn of the oak, was planted by the Prince of Wales in 2001 on the 350th anniversary of Charles's visit. It now grows alongside its parent tree.

FARM

Boscobel's farmyard, stretching around the north side of the house, is a well-preserved example of a 19th-century small 'planned farm'. Quiet and peaceful today, apart from a few tame ducks and chickens, it would once have been a busy, working farmyard.

A map of Boscobel from 1753 (see page 36) shows how the wooded landscape around the house had begun to change as advances in agriculture encouraged farmers to turn their woods into profitable farmland. New crops such as turnips were grown in fields around the house, and the oak was left at the tip of a strip of trees. The farm buildings at this date were still typical of the medieval farmstead: a large threshing barn, offset some short distance from the house; a long stabling barn; another building nearby; and what may have been a dovecote in the centre of the path between the buildings. The stabling barn survives, divided into two stables for working horses at the east end and a large cowhouse in the centre. Hay and straw were stowed above. The threshing barn in the field on the other side of the public road is now privately owned. It was rebuilt in red brick by Walter Evans in the 19th century.

Evans rebuilt the farmyard to the new 19th-century specifications of efficiency and productiveness. A compact and enclosed farmyard, with buildings facing into it and directly accessible from each other, eased tasks such as the collection of manure to spread on the fields. Farm labourers could also be kept hard at work. To expand dairy production Evans built

Above: The earliest farm building, the barn, in Boscobel farmyard. One of the two stables is open to visitors, as is the cowhouse in the centre
Below: A boat wagon, similar to that at Boscobel, being used to transport hay from the field to a hay rick in the farmyard. The 'ladder' at the front enabled the wagon to carry large loads, up to 2.5 tons

Right: One of the stables at Boscobel, used to house working horses. The hay and straw stored above helped keep the stalls warm for when the horses returned from work in the fields

Below: A dairy shorthorn heifer. When Boscobel's farm stock was sold at auction in 1918, lots included 83 head of shorthorn cattle (including a pedigree shorthorn bull) as well as '131 well-bred Shropshire sheep', and '7 valuable waggon horses'

Bottom: Boscobel's smithy, with its machinery still in working order

a new cowhouse in the centre of the farmyard, with a granary above. This was an unusual arrangement, as generally grain was kept away from animals for fear of spoiling. Pigs occupied sties near the gateway (now rebuilt as the shop). A cartshed protected valuable machinery from the weather (and animals), and alongside it, a set of brick buildings incorporated a bull pen (now public toilets), a henhouse and a smithy, which is still in working order with its late 19th-century equipment. A large Dutch barn for storing hay (dismantled in 1967) stood in what is now the car park.

At the back of the yard, the 19th-century carriage driveway to the house led through the white gate. Alongside it are hackney stables, which housed the driving horses.

◨ NORTH RANGE AND DAIRY

The western part of the north range was built in about 1595, but in about 1696 two eastern bays were added. The end bay was unheated and probably built for agricultural use. The other upper rooms were used as bedrooms, either for servants and children during the 19th century or for the tenant farmer's family in the 20th century. Smoke blackening from the 16th-century smoke-hood (an early type of chimney) can be seen against the wall in the first exhibition room upstairs.

During the 19th century, the whole ground floor of the north range became Boscobel's dairy. The western room was the settling room, lined with wide, shallow brick troughs. Cool water was pumped into the troughs and kept the milk fresh while the cream settled at the top of the ceramic pans. The stone trough was used to empty out the milk pans and equipment and store the cream pots. When dairy operations at Boscobel expanded to the barn complex over the road in the early 20th century, this room was used to salt pigs.

The scullery was in the middle of the north range; here the dairy maids made butter and cheese. The large boiling vat heated water to pass through the cheese vat and turn the cream into curds. A pipe leading across the farmyard took the waste whey from the cheese-making process and fed it to the pigs. The end room was used for pressing the cheese and forming the butter, and storing both until ready for market.

LOST BUILDINGS

Behind the north range, where only the footings remain in the ground, were the brewhouse and the bakehouse. An extension was built, probably in the 18th century, to link these buildings to the large kitchen, whose fireplace remains in the wall. The kitchen was linked to the north range at its western end. The buildings, which had fallen into ruin, were removed in 1969.

Above: Jug and butter pat in the dairy
Below: Boscobel's farmyard at the beginning of the 20th century

White Ladies Priory

Charles was attended at White Ladies by the Penderel brothers, but did not stay long inside, taking refuge instead in a wood nearby

The Priory

Founded around the mid-12th century as the priory of St Leonard at Brewood, White Ladies was an Augustinian house of canonesses. It was called White Ladies after the white habits of the nuns, and to distinguish it from the Benedictine house of Black Ladies, one mile away, also in the forest of Brewood. With only a modest income from its scattered properties, and no prominent lay patron, it has little recorded history. King John (r.1199–1216) took some interest in its fortunes, granting it a weir on the river Severn, near Bridgnorth, and some land exemptions in 1212, and further small grants were made by local families. In 1326, a nun of noble birth, Elizabeth la Zouche, from Ashby de la Zouche in Leicestershire, is recorded as escaping from the convent, but in 1332 she made confession before the bishop of Lichfield in Brewood church and was readmitted. In 1338, a charge of expensive dress, laxity and hunting with dogs was made against the prioress. In 1535, the priory's revenues were only £31 1s. 4d., and at the Suppression its buildings were said to be 'in great decay'. A year later, in 1536, it was included in the first wave of religious houses to be suppressed – those whose income totalled under £200 per annum.

A House at White Ladies

After the Suppression, the priory was leased to William Skeffington, who may have rebuilt some of the west range as a handsome, timber-framed house. Skeffington was buried in Tong church in 1550. By 1587, White Ladies was in the hands of Edward Giffard, who lived with his wife, Frances, in the house at White Ladies; a document of 1603 records the sale of one of Giffard's other properties, on the proviso that, as an old man, he 'does not have to travel over five miles from his house at White Ladies'. The house passed to Frances at his death, and her will of 1624 throws a little light on the contents: her eldest son,

Below: The ruins of White Ladies Priory from the south-east

John, was to receive the 'furnace now standing in the brewing house at White Ladies together with the cooler vats and other vessels and furniture for brewing and baking … and I also give to him the books in the study at White Ladies together with all the furniture of the said study'.

Charles at White Ladies

When Charles was brought to the house in 1651, John Giffard himself was dead. Accounts vary as to who was present at White Ladies during the king's visit but Giffard's widow, Dorothy, was still alive in 1654, and must have been the 'mistress Giffard' mentioned in the accounts, given special dispensation to remain in her house despite the fact that the land had been sequestered (confiscated). Charles was attended in the house by the Penderel brothers, but did not stay long inside, taking refuge instead in Spring Coppice, a wood nearby.

Later History

From the second half of the 17th century, White Ladies belonged to the Fitzherberts, along with Boscobel. The timber-framed house itself, however, was pulled down in the 18th century, and when the two estates of Boscobel and White Ladies were sold to the Evans family in 1812, Lord Stafford of Swynnerton, a descendant of the Fitzherberts, retained the priory church and the land adjoining it. The gatehouse survived into the 19th century, and was used to house farm labourers. The church at White Ladies remained a Catholic burial ground during the 18th and early 19th centuries, with the last interment in 1844.

Only the walls of the 12th-century priory church now remain at White Ladies. A fine Romanesque arch leads into the north transept. During the 19th century decorated medieval floor tiles were found at the site and old gravestones could still be seen. One was a copy of the one belonging to Joan Penderel (d.1669), who had protected the king at Boscobel, and another that of her son, William Penderel (d.1707).

White Ladies was given into guardianship by Lord Stafford in 1938. It can be visited in daylight hours and admission is free.

Above: Mary Barbara Huddleston, a nun at the English convent at Bruges, in about 1725, wearing the white habit of an Augustinian canoness. The nuns at White Ladies would have worn similar habits

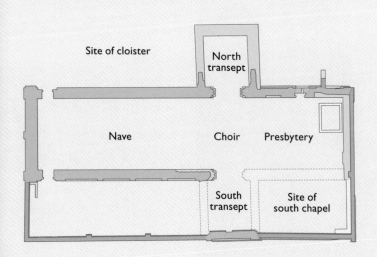

Site of cloister

North transept

Nave   Choir   Presbytery

South transept   Site of south chapel

N

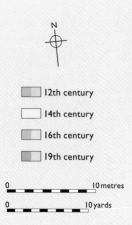

☐ 12th century

☐ 14th century

☐ 16th century

☐ 19th century

0 ――――――― 10 metres

0 ――――――― 10 yards

History

Built by John Giffard
some time before 1624,
Boscobel House was
only a few decades old
when it played a pivotal
role in the story of
Charles II. The future
king sought refuge here
after his defeat at the
battle of Worcester in
September 1651.
He was cared for by
the Penderel brothers,
servants of the Giffards.
After the Restoration
in 1660, Boscobel
remained in the hands
of the Fitzherberts,
descendants of the
Giffards, until 1812,
when it was bought
by Walter Evans, a
well-known cotton
manufacturer from
Derby. Sold by the
Evans family in 1918 to
the earl of Bradford, the
house was handed into
State guardianship in
1954, and the farmyard
in 1967.

Left: The tomb of John Giffard of
Chillington (d.1613), and his wife,
Joyce, in the church of St Mary and
St Chad in Brewood. He was the
elder brother of Edward Giffard of
Whiteladies (d.1606). Other tombs of
the Giffard family in the church date
from the 16th and 17th centuries
Below: The oldest part of the north
range, dated by tree-ring analysis
to 1595

Facing page: Cromwell's troops
searching for the king in Boscobel
wood, from a broadsheet illustration
of 1660

THE 16TH-CENTURY BUILDING

After Henry VIII's suppression of White Ladies Priory in 1536
(see page 20), the priory's land came into the hands of
Thomas Throckmorton, one of the most prominent Catholics
of the late 16th century. Throckmorton sold the White Ladies
estate to Edward Giffard, second son of John Giffard of
Chillington in Staffordshire, in 1587. In 1595, Giffard made over
the land to his wife, Frances Giffard, and it appears it was at
this date that the first building was erected on this site;
tree-ring analysis dates timbers in the north range to 1595.
The purpose of Giffard's first building is unclear. He called
himself 'Edward Giffard of White Ladies' and lived in the large
house at White Ladies, which had been converted from the
former priory's buildings. It is possible that this first building
at Boscobel, the west part of the north range, was simply a
woodsman's house, perhaps designed to provide the estate
with 'all manner of woods and trees', which he carefully
enunciates in his will.

BOSCOBEL HOUSE

When Edward Giffard died in 1606, his estate passed to his
widow, Frances Giffard. She herself died in 1625, and her
possessions were split between her children. John, her eldest
son, inherited the White Ladies estate as well as another
property in Blymhill, Staffordshire. In a document of 1624
John Giffard is named as 'John Giffard of Boscobel', indicating
that the house was built by this time, perhaps on the
understanding that he would soon also inherit his mother's
larger property at White Ladies. Thomas Blount, publishing
the first of the accounts of Charles's escape in 1660, writes
that Boscobel was built 'about thirty years before', suggesting
a date of about 1630. By 1632, the house was clearly already
built, as John Giffard was making his own arrangements for his
daughters to inherit 'the site of the house now called or knowne

The Giffard Family and Catholic Persecution

The Giffards resisted the new Protestantism of the 16th century and continued to practise their Catholicism in private

The Giffard family had owned land at Chillington since 1178; during the Middle Ages they were one of the most prominent landed families in Staffordshire. Like many of the gentry, they quietly resisted the new Protestantism of the 16th century and continued to practise their Catholicism in private. When Queen Elizabeth I (r.1558–1603) visited Staffordshire in 1575 – one of her more recalcitrant territories – John Giffard at Chillington was an obvious host. The queen's visit, however, was disastrous for the Giffards: they were denounced as Catholics and within three days John Giffard was summoned to appear before the Privy Council. He was either in prison or on parole until his death in 1613. It was a salutary lesson. From this point the Giffards were careful to cultivate their loyalty to the monarch while maintaining a secret network of Catholics loyal to themselves.

The persecution of Catholics in the 17th century peaked in the wake of the Gunpowder Plot of 1605, during Cromwell's Commonwealth from 1649 to 1660, and between 1678 and 1679 after false revelations by Titus Oates (a priest and perjurer) about a 'Catholic plot'. Catholics' land was seized and those who did not attend Anglican services, called recusants, were heavily fined. No Catholic could hold public office and any Catholic priest found was imprisoned and could be executed. In 1654, Dorothy Giffard, the widow of the John Giffard who built Boscobel, petitioned for the return of part of her land, which had been confiscated because she was a Catholic. After the Restoration, the Giffards benefited temporarily from their role in Charles's escape, but their descendants were still persecuted well into the 18th century. Despite this, the area around Brewood had the strongest concentration of Catholics in Staffordshire. The church of St Mary and St Chad at Brewood contains some very fine early Giffard tombs (see page 23).

Above: Elizabethan anti-Catholic allegory satirizing the Catholic mass. The bishops, shown as foxes, are getting 'drunk on the blood of martyrs'
Right: The destruction of a Catholic chapel, depicted in an illustration of 1646. Despite persecution, the Giffards continued to keep a priest at Chillington Hall; in 1715 he was being paid £50 per annum. The chapel plate included 'a large gold chalice', 'six large silver candlesticks', and 'a large silver crucifix'

by the name of Boscobell'. Only one daughter, Frances, was in fact to survive him.

Giffard's choice of location for his new house is interesting. Although traditionally called a hunting lodge, the house may have had less to do with hunting than the life of the Catholic gentry in the 17th century. No park has been found associated with the house, although there were parks nearby. There is no mention of hunting in 17th-century contemporary accounts, nor of any related role for William Penderel, caretaker at Boscobel in 1651. Giffard had no sons, but three daughters, two of whom predeceased him. He himself appears to have been a Catholic intellectual. As a young man he spent time in France, and he was a close family friend of Basil Brooke (1576–1646), a leading Catholic activist. Brooke was an innovative figure, connected to James I and Charles I, an entrepreneur in the mining and smelting industry, a Catholic devotional writer and campaigner. Like Brooke, Giffard maintained strong Catholic ties. The early 17th century was still a period of active religious persecution; not only were recusants (those who did not attend Anglican church services) fined and penalized but Catholic gatherings of any sort were regarded with especial alarm. Boscobel's discreet location would have ensured privacy for the family and for Giffard's gentry friends.

By 1651, however, John Giffard was dead and his widow and surviving daughter were living at White Ladies. Boscobel was occupied only by William Penderel and his wife, Joan – loyal Catholic family servants. It was during a few days in early September 1651 that the fortunes of the house changed.

Above: The earliest illustration of Boscobel and White Ladies, by Wenceslaus Hollar, published in Blount's account of 1660

Below: Sir Basil Brooke, whose house at Madeley was 14 miles from Boscobel. At Giffard's housewarming feast Brooke was invited to name the house, calling it Boscobel, from the Italian 'bosco bello', meaning beautiful wood

S. Bazill Brooke

Above: An early 18th-century portrait of Oliver Cromwell, possibly by Jonathan Richardson, which hangs in the parlour at Boscobel
Below: Detail of an eyewitness painting of the execution of King Charles I in 1649, by the Flemish painter John Weesop

CIVIL WAR AND THE EVENTS OF 1651

Although Charles I (r.1625–49) had come to the throne in an era of relative peace, his marriage to a Catholic princess, Henrietta Maria, alarmed Protestants, and was exacerbated by his High Anglicanism. His belief in the 'divine right of kings' and his failure to call Parliament for a decade antagonized the English nobility. In 1640, financial pressure forced him to call a new Parliament, but it immediately proposed reforms and polarized opinion in the country. Civil War finally broke out in 1642 between Royalists and Parliamentarians and on 30 January 1649 Charles I was beheaded in Whitehall, on a charge of treason.

Oliver Cromwell dominated the subsequent Commonwealth of England. He was a committed Puritan and led massacres of Catholics in Ireland. In 1650 Cromwell was fighting in Ireland when the young Charles, son of Charles I, who had fled to France four years earlier, landed in Scotland to try to regain the throne. Despite a disappointing reception, Charles was crowned king of Scotland at Scone and marched south with 14,000 Scottish troops. Cromwell swiftly returned from Ireland and pursued him. The young king moved through Lancashire, hoping to capitalize on Royalist sympathies in the west, but when the two armies finally met at Worcester on 3 September 1651, Charles's troops were tired and outnumbered and they were no match for Cromwell's 28,000 men. The Royalists were decisively defeated, with 5,000 men dead or captured.

As the Stuart heir to a country in turmoil, Charles remained a significant threat. Parliament immediately issued proclamations and rewards for the arrest of 'the traitor', and patrols of soldiers spread out urgently to search for him.

Shropshire in the Civil War

From 1642 to 1651, England was at war. The Midlands saw some of the worst of the fighting, as the area was divided between supporters of Parliament and the king. The first and last field battles of Edgehill and Worcester were fought in the region. The turbulence of these years virtually destroyed Shropshire's economy and disrupted civilian life. Men left home to fight, leaving their crops and families unprotected. Towns and villages were plundered by both sides and stocks of food and materials were seized. Rents could not be collected, markets shut down and trade virtually ceased, as goods were intercepted by parties of soldiers. Civilians had to obtain an official pass to make even the shortest journey by road, and request a permit to stay overnight. The roads became empty of traffic, except for marching troops, who often fanned out across adjacent fields, trampling crops as they went. By the end of the war, most families had lost relatives and often much of their land, and men who returned were frequently wounded and unable to work.

After the Restoration, Charles II received petitions from those who had suffered in the Civil War. One who hoped for special favour was Mary Graves, who had looked after the family of Francis Yates, Charles's guide to White Ladies, after his death: 'your petitioner hath ever since been forced to keep his wife and five children … for so doing she hath been utterly ruined'. Charles was sympathetic, and Mary received financial assistance.

> The turbulence of these years virtually destroyed Shropshire's economy and disrupted civilian life

Left: The battle of Worcester, 3 September 1651, depicted in a commemorative broadsheet of 1660. Cromwell's troops closed in on the town from three sides, pursuing the Royalists through the streets. Charles was forced to flee via St Martin's Gate, shown at the top left of the picture

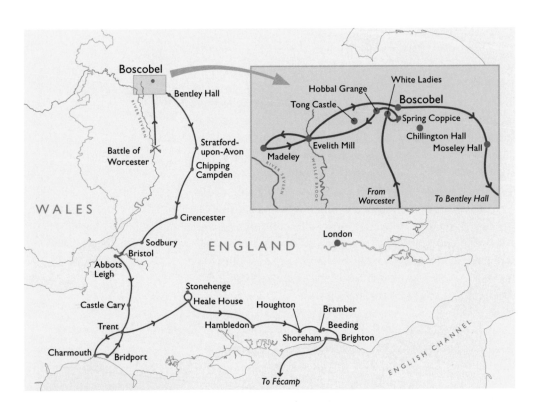

Top: A map showing Charles's escape route after the battle of Worcester

Above: A portrait of the diarist Samuel Pepys in 1666, by John Hayls. Pepys first listened to Charles's account of his escape on board the ship returning him to England in 1660. Twenty years later, Pepys was invited to take down the king's account in detail

FLIGHT FROM WORCESTER

The story of Charles's escape spread around England after the Restoration, and the king encouraged it. Several narrative accounts were recorded, but the first one was published in 1660 by Thomas Blount, a lawyer and a Catholic. In 1680, the king dictated his own account to Samuel Pepys. This guidebook draws on these two sources, plus other first-hand accounts collected by Pepys. A few details and timings remain uncertain, but the account is generally consistent. It remains one of the most vivid and remarkable stories in English history.

Exhausted by five hours of desperate fighting, Charles and several hundred of his troops escaped north from Worcester as darkness fell. Charles consulted urgently with his companions, but found them panicked and 'mightily distracted'. Rather than try to get back to Scotland, he hoped to turn and reach London before his pursuers, but knew he needed to shake off his troops: 'though I could not get them to stand by me against the enemy, I could not get rid of them now I had a mind to it'. He confided his plan to his closest companion, Lord Wilmot. Sixty men, 'gentlemen and officers', managed to slip away off the high road. They rode silently through a nearby town, as Cromwell's militia waited unsuspecting nearby. Charles consulted his companions to see where they might take a few hours' rest. The earl of Derby suggested Boscobel House, a place of 'great convenience of concealment', in which he had himself taken refuge earlier that summer. He 'acquainted the king it was a recusant's house; and it was suggested, that those people (being accustomed to persecution and searches) were most like to have the readiest means and safest contrivances to preserve him: his majesty therefore inclined to go thither'. Charles Giffard, one of the Royalist officers (and son of the Giffards of Chillington), was brought forward to lead the way. The party stopped briefly at a house near Stourbridge and, as they rode on, the king asked further about Boscobel. Giffard proposed going first to White Ladies, where Charles would be able to rest and make plans.

CHARLES AT WHITE LADIES

Charles arrived at White Ladies at daybreak. He knew only that 'it was a private house that Mr Giffard, who was a Staffordshire-man, had told me belonged to honest people that lived thereabouts'. George Penderel, a 'servant of the house', ushered them in. The group gathered in the hall and Giffard sent for Richard Penderel, the eldest brother, who lived at Hobbal Grange. A boy, Bartholomew Martin, was sent to collect William Penderel. Meanwhile, 'Mistress Giffard' (probably Dorothy Giffard, John Giffard's elderly widow) 'brought his majesty some sack [dry white wine] and biscuit'.

News came of the Scottish troops: 3,000 were gathered on the heath next to Tong Castle, still under their commander, David Leslie, but 'all in disorder'. Pursuers were closing in, and Charles saw his only chance of escape: 'This made me take the resolution of putting my selfe into a disguise, and endeavouring to gett a foote to London in a country-fellowes habbit, with a

Above: A portrait of Charles II as a young man, in about 1648, after Adriaen Hanneman
Below: Richard Penderel helps Charles with his disguise, in a 17th-century painting by Isaac Fuller. This is one of a series of five paintings made after the Restoration to commemorate the events of 1651

Above: Boscobel with the Royal Oak, c.1670, commissioned by King Charles II from Robert Streater. On the left is White Ladies, which has just been searched by Parliamentarian troops; the house at White Ladies, in which Charles took brief refuge, is in the centre; and Boscobel House is on the right, hidden in dense woodland

Below: Richard Penderel, William Careless and Charles, in Boscobel wood in a 17th-century painting by Isaac Fuller

pair of ordinary grey cloath britches, a leathern dublett and a greene jerkin … I also cutt my haire very short, and flung my cloathes into a privy-house, that noe boddy might see that any boddy had beene stripping themselves.' His companions left to join Leslie, hoping they might escape to Scotland. They begged the king not to divulge his plans, knowing what torture could await them.

His face and hands rubbed with soot from the fire, Charles was led by Richard Penderel out of the back door and into a wood nearby, called Spring Coppice. There he 'stayed all day without meate or drinke', and 'by great good fortune it rained all the time, which hindered them, as I believe, from comeing (into the wood) to search for men that might be fledd hither'.

CHARLES ATTEMPTS TO REACH WALES

The plan to reach London was abandoned. Penderel knew of no safe-houses on the way, and Charles now thought it too obvious a route. He resolved to make for Wales, where he could take a trading ship from Swansea to France. 'Besides, that I remembered severall honest gentlemen that were of my acquaintance in Whales.' Barely rested and still hardly fed, the two left on foot as soon as it was dark, stopping only briefly at Hobbal Grange to improve Charles's disguise. Penderel urged the king not to speak if approached, for fear of his accent betraying him.

Reaching Evelith Mill, ten miles away, around midnight, they saw the miller sitting outside the mill-house, his white clothes

just visible in the dark. 'Who goes there?' he called. 'Neighbours going home', answered Penderel. 'If you be neighbours, stand, or I will knock you downe!' The two ran, pursued by men rushing out of the mill. 'Rogues, rogues!' called out the miller, as Penderel and his companion escaped down a lane, leapt over a hedge and lay, listening, until danger had passed.

At dawn they reached a house belonging to a Mr Woolfe at Madeley. Charles waited 'under a hedge by a greate tree', while Penderel enquired whether Woolfe would shelter a fugitive from the battle of Worcester. Woolfe refused, as it was 'so dangerous a thing', unless it was the king himself. Penderel told him it was.

Woolfe told the king that his house had been searched and his hiding places discovered. The fugitives were taken to Woolfe's barn instead, where they ate some cold meat and spent the day, concealed 'behinde his corne and hay'. Conferring that evening with Woolfe's son, they learned that the militia were in town and all routes over the Severn were heavily guarded.

London seemed the only possibility and the two set out to return to 'Penderells-house' that night. Avoiding the miller this time, they reached the river bank. Penderel could not swim, but Charles 'entering the river first to see whither I could my selfe goe over, who knew how to swim, found it was but a little above my middle; and thereupon takeing Richard Penderell by the hand, I helped him over'.

Below: A portrait of Richard Penderel, who helped Charles at Boscobel and travelled with him to Madeley and back. The eldest of the Penderel brothers, he lived at Hobbal Grange at the time of Charles's visit

A Reconstruction Drawing of Boscobel in 1651

*An artist's reconstruction of Boscobel on the evening of 6 September 1651.
Charles has spent the day in the oak tree, and is sitting at the parlour table,
while Joan Penderel brings him a dish of chicken. William Careless sits alongside
him. Humphrey Penderel arrives with news of the search at White Ladies*

A The plainer north range was built about 30 years before the lodge

B The original stack was taller than it is today and served large fireplaces
in the basement, ground and first floors

C The attic floor was originally lit by dormers on both sides; these were
removed in the 18th century

D The original first-floor chamber was as big as the ground-floor parlour
is today

CHARLES AT BOSCOBEL

The two bedraggled men arrived at Boscobel at dawn. They had walked miles through two nights and had hardly slept or eaten. Charles was brought into the house, where he met a local Royalist officer, Major William Careless, also a fugitive from Worcester. Joan Penderel, William's wife, 'made his majesty a posset of thin milk and small beer, and got ready some warm water to wash his feet, not only extremely dirty, but much galled with travel'. His shoes, 'full of gravel', and his stockings 'which were very wet', were removed and 'there being no other shoes in the house that would fit him, the good-wife put some hot embers in those to dry them'. Charles 'ate bread and cheese heartily' at the parlour table.

Careless warned Charles that neither the house nor the wood was safe, for they would certainly be searched. There was 'only one way how to pass the next day, and that was to get up into a greate oake in a pretty plain place, where we might see round about us'. Helped up by William and Richard Penderel, and carrying a parcel of food for the day, 'bread, cheese, small beere', Charles and Careless climbed into a large oak that had been cut back a few years before 'and being growne out again very bushy and thick, could nott be seene through.' There they stayed the whole day. Charles slept fitfully, his head, it is said, resting in Careless's lap. Later, the king remembered: 'while we were in this tree, we see soldiers goeing up and downe in the thickest of the wood, searching for persons escaped, we seeing them now and then peeping out of the woods.'

That evening they returned to the house. Charles was shown the hiding place previously used by the earl of Derby; he was shaved and his hair was cut shorter. Humphrey Penderel, the miller of White Ladies, arrived with news that the militia had searched White Ladies after the king's visit, threatened him with the penalty for harbouring the king ('death without mercy') and reminded him of the reward for disclosure: one thousand pounds. Humphrey had remained silent and had been dismissed, but the panelling in the house had been ripped up. Joan Penderel served Charles some chicken while the Penderels kept watch. Charles was put to bed in a hiding place, on 'a little pallet'.

The king awoke early the next morning, walked a little in the 'gallery' which had 'the advantage of a window which surveyed the road from Tong to Brewood', and said some prayers. His hiding place had been cramped and bare and he was relieved to escape it. William Penderel had gone out and taken a sheep from a neighbour's sheepcot, and Careless had killed it with a dagger. Charles then called for a knife and sliced the leg up into chops and the two of them breakfasted on 'Scotch collops', the king helping fry them himself. Later that day, he 'spent some part of this Lord's day in reading, in a pretty arbour in Boscobel garden, which grew upon a mount'.

Above: A 19th-century engraving of Charles in the oak tree at Boscobel

Mr Iane Lane and King:

the Kings escape m the sea Adventure.

Top: Charles riding in disguise as 'William Jackson' with Jane Lane, in a 17th-century engraving
Above: Charles finally left England by boat on 15 October 1651
Below: Portrait of Father John Huddleston, who sheltered Charles at Moseley after he left Boscobel

THE JOURNEY FROM BOSCOBEL

Charles left Boscobel as day faded on Sunday evening. A plan had been made for him to continue his journey dressed as an attendant to Mrs Jane Lane, a neighbour, who had a parliamentary pass to visit her pregnant cousin in Bristol. Charles was escorted to Moseley Hall, riding on Humphrey Penderel's old mill-horse. At Moseley the king took leave of the five Penderel brothers and was taken in by Thomas Whitgreave, a Catholic gentleman and friend of the Giffards, and Father John Huddleston, a Catholic priest. From Moseley, the king set out riding with Jane Lane. It was to be a journey of six weeks, in almost constant danger.

Travelling to Stratford-upon-Avon, Jane Lane's horse lost a shoe, and the king, in disguise as her manservant, took the animal to the blacksmith. As Charles later recalled, he asked the smith if there was any news. 'No news since the good news of the beating of the Scots.' 'Were any of the English taken with the Scots?' 'Some I heard were taken, but I did not hear that that rogue Charles Stuart was taken.' 'If that rogue were taken he deserved to be hanged, more than all the rest for bringing in the Scots,' answered Charles.

Jane Lane and Charles continued towards Cirencester, then to Bristol. Meeting a fugitive from Worcester, again Charles diverted suspicion by asking what kind of man the king was. As he later recounted, the description was accurate, but 'lookeing upon me he told me that the king was at least three fingers taller than I. I made what haste I could out of the buttery, for fear he should indeed know me.'

No ship could be found at Bristol leaving within the month so Charles continued into Dorset. A ship promised from Lyme Regis failed to arrive. The king was forced to stay at an inn full of Cromwell's soldiers at Bridport: 'I alighted, and taking the horses thought it the best way to go blundering in among them, and lead them through the middle of the soldiers into the stable, which I did and they were very angry with me for my rudeness.'

Eventually, he reached Shoreham-on-Sea, near Brighton. Taken on a ship full of unsuspecting merchantmen, he reached Rouen. From there, he travelled to Paris and the safety of the royal court of Louis XIV.

THE RESTORATION

The story of Boscobel and the Royal Oak became a central part of the celebrations at Charles's Restoration as king on 29 May 1660. The date, the king's 30th birthday, was designated 'Oak Apple Day' and a public holiday. Enthusiasm for the story was genuine. For the king, it proclaimed the loyalty of his subjects and his own heroism and triumph. For his subjects, who had been battered by decades of civil war and harsh Puritan laws, the story and the oak itself became symbols of fresh hope and optimism.

Boscobel became a precious part of Catholic folklore. Still under threat of persecution, a group of Catholics held a secret ceremony at the house one night in August 1678 to inaugurate a Jesuit priest. Dozens of recusant gentry attended the ceremony, and the party then went out to view the oak, followed by a dinner of venison at the house, at which the king's health was drunk.

The king rewarded those who had helped him. The Penderels each received a life pension in perpetuity, which is still administered today by the Giffards of Chillington, although eroded by inflation. Charles Giffard received a life pension. In 1658 William Careless joined the king in the Netherlands and the king formally changed his name to Carlos, granting him a coat of arms depicting an oak tree with three crowns. Thomas Whitgreave was rewarded with a life pension. A grant for annuity was paid to the widow of Francis Yates, who had escorted Charles to White Ladies. Jane Lane became lady-in-waiting to the king's sister and received a payment of £1,000. John Huddleston, the Catholic priest at Moseley, who had become a Benedictine monk, was invited by Charles to live at Somerset House under the protection of the dowager queen, Henrietta Maria. In 1685, at Charles's own death, Father Huddleston is said to have received the king into the Catholic faith.

Above: A portrait of Jane Lane after the Restoration; she accompanied Charles on his six-week journey from Boscobel

Below: Detail of the coronation procession of Charles II from Westminster to the Tower of London, 22 April 1661, by Dirck Stoop

Above: The striking farmhouse wing, dating from the 18th and 19th centuries, and painted during the 19th century to match the older timber-framed parts of the house

Below: Copy of a map of the Boscobel estate, from 1753. The house is at the bottom of the map; the present public road follows the line of the track seen running between the farm buildings

BOSCOBEL IN THE 17TH AND 18TH CENTURIES

By the late 17th century, Boscobel was in the hands of the Fitzherbert family. John Giffard's daughter, Frances, had married John Cotton in 1633, and later their daughter, Jane, inherited the Boscobel and White Ladies estate, with her husband, Basil Fitzherbert. The Fitzherberts were themselves Catholic landed gentry; their main seat was at Swynnerton, near Stone in Staffordshire. Basil and Jane cared for Boscobel, building a brick wall around the Royal Oak and perhaps

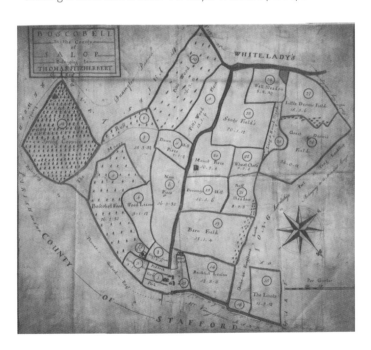

carrying out some of the later 17th-century alterations. During the 18th century Boscobel and its estate remained in Fitzherbert ownership, but were successively tenanted out to yeoman farmers.

Boscobel was visited by a number of well-known antiquarians throughout the 18th century, such as William Stukeley in 1712. A letter to the *Gentleman's Magazine* in 1790 noted that visitors were received kindly: the occupants of the house 'have always shown a proper attention to every curious stranger and a kind hospitality within-doors, when a politeness of behaviour entitled those strangers to distinction'.

Those visiting at the end of the 18th century were surprised, however, to find the oak not in the midst of a dense wood, but at the edge of a more open landscape. John Byng, later 5th Viscount Torrington, visited in 1792, and spoke to the tenant farmer, John Lockley: 'all the wood to the left, and about the oak, was fell'd and grubb'd up by me last year', said Lockley, 'it was quite like a forest – and so again behind the house. But I left the tree – will you walk to it?'

BOSCOBEL IN THE 19TH CENTURY

In 1810, the Fitzherbert family put the Boscobel and White Ladies estates up for sale. At 659 acres (267 ha) of prime farmland, meadows, pasture and woodland, the estates were an excellent prospect for an ambitious farmer keen to make the most of a fall in land prices. Industrialists across England were buying up similar land and Walter Evans, a rich and enterprising cotton manufacturer from Darley Abbey in Derbyshire, was attracted by Boscobel's romantic link with the fugitive king.

The sale was delayed because of legal negotiations with Boscobel's tenant, and by 1812 the farm buildings had deteriorated. Evans bartered over the price, but in October 1812 he bought Boscobel and White Ladies estates for his two unmarried stepdaughters, Frances and Elizabeth.

The 19th-century history of Boscobel, as a house lovingly restored by the Evans family and a romantic family enterprise, is as much part of Boscobel's story as the story of the fleeing king. Walter Evans, his wife and daughters Frances, Elizabeth and Ellen, studied the 17th- and 18th-century illustrations of the house, and refurbished the interior·in an antiquarian style to look 'as it was when Charles was there'. It was also made more comfortable, the fireplace in the Squire's Room was opened up, bookcases were inserted and the old casement windows were replaced with 'Gothick' sash windows. The family remained at Darley Abbey but visited frequently. They established four local schools and sent over bank clerks from Derby to train 'the best of the cottage women' as teachers. When Frances died in 1875, Elizabeth, her older sister, inherited the house, and was still visiting from Derby in her

Top: Frances Evans, who was given Boscobel House by her stepfather Walter Evans in 1812
Above: Elizabeth Evans, who was given White Ladies, and inherited Boscobel after her sister's death in 1875

Above: *Cotton thread from the Evans factories in Darley Abbey was exported all over Europe*

Right: *A photograph of the Evans family enjoying the sunshine in the garden at Boscobel in the mid-19th century. On the right is 'Great Aunt Bessy', possibly Elizabeth Evans*

Below: *Edward Elgar, the composer, visited Boscobel in July 1897. He 'went all over the old house' and spent 'a very jolly day' flying kites in the field near the Royal Oak*

eighties, evidently an intriguing sight. One of Boscobel's occupants later wrote: 'She drove all the way in a huge yellow carriage with a pair of great fat carriage horses, an exact match, with lovely satiny skins. Her coachman was 80, she herself much over 80, and her maid nearly as old. Imagine them – they looked the very personification of immensely rich old age. She was a tiny dainty little lady, dressed always in rich old-fashioned silk, a beautiful lace scarf over her shoulders, and heaps of glittering trinkets which tinkled as she moved.'

By the later 19th century, the Victorian appetite for romantic history, along with the new Midlands railway, brought streams of visitors to the house. The tenant farmer's wife acted as a custodian and, when the family was not in residence, offered the lodge as a 'show-house', taking visitors around for a small gratuity. Day-trippers and school-parties came from Wolverhampton; national dignitaries, including Disraeli and the future Queen Mary, were brought along in house-parties of the local aristocracy.

Boscobel's farm, meanwhile, prospered. The north range was converted to dairy production and its butter and cheese were sold in local markets.

Memories of Boscobel

Richard Marsh, born at nearby Shifnal in 1937, recalls life at Boscobel as a tenant farmer until 1967.

'Boscobel was a fantastic place to live, as it was easy to get to places: Wolverhampton, Albrighton, Cosford and Brewood weren't far away. I never went to school much myself, but I learned all about the place because I lived with it for so many years.

'The king and queen came to visit in 1942. I was only five at the time, so I had to stay inside, though I was allowed to look out of the bedroom window upstairs. They only told us the day before that they were coming. I think it was three or four cars that came. They looked all around the house, and then went out to the oak. My parents used to talk about it afterwards; it was quite a thing to have happened.

'We farmed 282 acres at Boscobel. We kept sheaves of corn in the Dutch barn until it was time for threshing them, then the corn was stored in the granary, mostly in sacks. We sold our milk to Midland County Dairies, in Wolverhampton. It went by lorry and churn. The churns were put on the back of the lorries, 11-gallon churns; it had been 17-gallon churns at one time. After 1939 we milked the other side of the road. They stopped making cheese at Boscobel in 1932.

'We had two farmhands in the end, but at one time we had seven or eight – a cowman, general labourers, a tractor driver. We had three horses when I was little, Shire horses, not riding horses though. We had 50 pigs at the most and they went to market. We killed a pig every year and cured the bacon.

'We had prisoners-of-war at Boscobel too: the Italians came first, then German prisoners. Then came displaced persons from Poland. They worked on the land. They all spoke broken English but they had translation books with them. They were keen to learn, even as a lad I remember they were keen, because they were thinking of staying. They were quite keen gardeners too.'

> 'The king and queen came to visit in 1942. I was only five at the time, so I had to stay inside'

Above: Richard Marsh as a young boy with his sister at Boscobel
Left: King George VI and Queen Elizabeth at the Royal Oak in 1942

*Above: Boscobel House from its
19th-century entrance*
*Below: The Prince of Wales visited
Boscobel in 2001 on the 350th
anniversary of Charles II's visit. He
planted an oak sapling, grown from
an acorn of the Royal Oak, beside
the parent tree*

MODERN-DAY BOSCOBEL

By the end of the 19th century, the Evans's responsibility for
a house far from the family base in Derbyshire had become a
strain. Ill-feeling had also developed between the family and
Boscobel's long-standing tenant farmers, Thomas and Sarah
Brown. Walter Evans's granddaughter wrote of her
exasperation with Mrs Brown in particular: 'the beautiful old
blankets embroidered in the corners are riddled with moth, a
great deal of the linen is gone. She complained bitterly if Father
lent the house to any relation to stay in, made herself most
disagreeable to us over it and charged exorbitantly.'

Prospects for land values were bleak and in 1913 the family
put the house up for sale. The estate was bought eventually in
1918 by the earl of Bradford, of Weston Park in Staffordshire.
Boscobel's contents were either sold at auction or dispersed to
other Evans properties. The portraits of Charles and Cromwell,
along with Dame Joan Penderel's spinning wheel and the old
dining table at which Charles had eaten in 1651, were sold in
London under the title 'a nation's heirlooms'.

The house remained open to visitors under Lord Bradford's
ownership, though the rooms were left largely bare. In 1954,
Lord Bradford placed the house in the guardianship of the
Ministry of Works. In 1967 the farm equipment, cattle and
horses were sold off by the tenant farmer, Richard Marsh.

The old pig sties and Dutch barn were pulled down by
the Ministry of Works, as well as the brewhouse and kitchen
at the back of the house, which were in a poor state of repair.
In 1988, English Heritage refurnished the house to its
appearance in about 1900 and in 2010 the dairy interiors and
the stables were restored.